STAYING RIGHT HERE

PRAISE FOR *STAYING RIGHT HERE*

Navigating the rise of American fascism after 9/11, *Staying Right Here* is a collection that delivers on its promise with each poem documenting the hard-won fight to find safety and stability in a world built against you. Hameedi's debut explores intergenerational trauma, diaspora, and identity while tracing a path between Pakistan, New York City, and Boston, asking what does it mean to stay, and what must we leave behind?

—Simone Person, author of *Smoke Girl*

Usman Hameedi's debut poetry collection is a complex and nuanced love letter to "a place beyond place." A fierce defense of home and how that concept changes when the forces of gentrification, space, and time push to alter it. These poems provide a window into critical junctures of Hameedi's life, where family, friends, and inspirations were first cast into their molten cores. From the vibrant Brooklyn streets that paved his childhood, to intimate moments shared with Abbu and Ammi, Hameedi illustrates with masterful clarity the heart and hustle of a young Pakistani boy's journey from unknowing child to seasoned poet, student of the game, and faithful son. These poems deserve to be held tight, studied closely, and read like the prayers they are.   **—Michael "Mic" Ting, 2018 Individual World Poetry Slam Champion, author of *Novelty***

Usman Hameedi's *Staying Right Here* is part love letter, part homage and part elegy to the cities and people we love. Full of tenderness and grief, Hameedi writes with the unflinching generosity of a poet who is holding "all the people I love / as if they were glass / butterfly wings."

—Noor Hindi, author of *Dear God. Dear Bones. Dear Yellow.*

Staying Right Here is a resolution against not only erasure, but against colonialism in its slipperiest form; compelled self-erasure. Usman Hameedi's poems identify resistance as an heirloom that lives in the classroom, the neighborhood deli, the mirror, a black & white photo of two lovers; it is a living thing among "unwieldy ruins" but, Hameedi asserts, "I will be the home I need." This collection is about what we lose, what we sacrifice—yes, but also what we reclaim, what we scream, what burns its way into belonging.

—Jay Ward, author of *Composition*

STAYING RIGHT HERE

Poems by

USMAN HAMEEDI

BUTTON PUBLISHING INC.

MINNEAPOLIS

2023

STAYING RIGHT HERE
POETRY
AUTHOR: Usman Hameedi
COVER DESIGN: Talisa Almonte
AUTHOR PHOTO: Beau

◆

◆

Published by Button Poetry
Minneapolis, MN 55418 | http://www.buttonpoetry.com

◆

Manufactured in the United States of America
PRINT ISBN: 978-1-63834-100-0
EBOOK ISBN: 978-1-63834-062-1
AUDIOBOOK ISBN: 978-1-63834-069-0

First printing

"There is no normal. There's just us,
and what we do with what we've been given."

—KAMALA KHAN, MS. MARVEL

For anyone who couldn't see themselves in the stories they read.
I hope my words mean something to you
and inspire you to write your own.

CONTENTS

STAYING RIGHT HERE

PREFACE

GOD BLESS DELI SPEAKS TO MY GENTRIFIED NEIGHBORHOOD

Don't you dare Columbus us,
call us a hidden gem, Buzzfeed us
into a new taste for unfamiliar mouths.

You cannot discover
what's already rooted,
flourishing before you arrived.
We've been here:
bearded, black hair, Yemeni.

Assalamualaikum! Keif al-Hal?
Been Muslim. Still Muslim—
before, during, and after 9/11.
Always halal and
to this day still delicious.

Brother Alex is on the grill,
a stainless-steel Sahara.
Watch the oil dance
like it was Eid-al Fitr.

Steam rises like the Adhan,
and we recite the Hadith of old New York City.
Takbir to the eggandcheeseonarollsaltpepperketchup,
the chicken cutlet on a hero,
the 2 for 5 specials.
The pilgrimage of chopped-cheese into toasted bread
while the aroma of lamb over rice
spills out of Styrofoam.

So good,
we can make a conservative Baptist
say Mashallah!

So come, Yallah!
Build
your bodega app,
your Subway restaurant,
your artisanal bread shop,
your overpriced replicated mediocrity—
whatever you wish.

Just understand
that our pepper sauce melts plexiglass.
We have seasoned our French Fries
with the salt of bigoted tears since 2001.

Born of arid Earth,
a life of heat and detonation,
God Bless is our oasis of opportunity.
You are most welcome,
but best believe,

Habibi,
we plan on staying
right here.

PART I:
HOME

CALCULUS

Shiny red Power Ranger
right by the cashier.
The store did that on purpose.

How could I ignore Jason
in crimson calling me
to join his next mission?

It's Morphin' Time!

Rita Repulsa and her army
of handed-down toys, old Beanie Babies
were threatening to destroy my room
and the world. Only we could stop them!

I wanted it. My own
toy, hero, storyline.
$20 at most.
Just one of those green bills.

No, Ammi said.
Not right now.

I was upset.
Heat in my face,
I grew redder
than the toy I wanted.

Too little to understand
my mother's arithmetic.

Just *one*
$20 bill
meant a few hours of factory work.
400 plastic bottles, 5 cents each
at the recycling machine.
Enough to buy
bread, milk, and eggs.

Ammi needed to make the choice
between a temper tantrum
and a hungry belly.

She was the superhero
I had by my side
the whole time.

With just one $20 bill,
she wove us a safety net.
Stable fridge full enough
to power a young boy's
growing imagination.

HEIRLOOM

My uncle died with molasses blood.
Leg swollen into a sugar cane bundle.
Foot rotting, blackened banana,
sap leaking from limbs.

He's the maple that didn't drip too far
from the scarred family tree.
He joined the family plot, a graveyard
with granulated-crystal tombstones.

Not sure who had it first, but I know
we are a family of patients.
Passed down from generations
are honey-filled veins,
hemoglobin frosted with glucose.

Syrup sinks in water
but still crosses continents.

Here in America,
Ammi wept saltwater
when her brother died. Reminisced
on how barfi-sweet he was,
a smile and laugh
memorable like dessert.

Then, she followed her own routine,
pricked her finger to feed the glucose monitor.

I have never known Abbu
living without insulin.
He taught me the proper injection procedure:
hold a syringe, give a patient a second chance.
Offered himself as clinical exposure
for medical school applications.

The more I kept learning about
medicine and my family,
I couldn't help but wonder if
he was also preparing me
for when our heirloom
eventually becomes my own.

CLOSED GATES

Ammi and I were outside of the store. Don't know where or what but
I remember waiting for Abbu. It was nighttime. I held Ammi's hand,
the both of us standing on the shadowed sidewalk below a stardust of
streetlights.

The storefront's heavy metal gates came down. A methodical descent,
low-baritone humming. Then, a loud clang as they bounced off the
concrete. The lights went out one by one.

I ran over to someone—maybe a security guard or a complete
stranger. Steel-chain tears descended—

Wait, wait, wait!
My dad is still there!
You can't close the store!
How will he get out—

and then Abbu appeared
from the other entrance.

That night, I learned
that buildings have multiple doors,
and Abbu's warm sweater
is the scent of home.

He knows I love him.
From hugs, phone calls, coming back home,
spending time with him.

But we barely know each other.
We live behind gates
I've put up.
Unnecessary boundaries
I drew.

I'm not sure why
it's still surface-level.
I could blame being brown—
That's just how brown dads and sons are—

But that isn't true.
Maybe as I grew up,
I learned that holding back
your love means you won't
be a mess when love is gone.
Can't cry over missing love
that never was.

I have so much
to unlearn.

I do know
I've taken for granted
Abbu coming back to hold me,
him always being there.

I love him so much.
But the number of times I've told him
could be held
in the palms of a child.

NYC SESTINA

No Metropolis can compare to The City.
Glittered solar flares embedded into each spotlight.
The footsteps, Versace to Nike, pound the cracked concrete.
Millions walk with the infamous fast pace,
the metronome of life.
This dirty elegance I'd never change, my home.

Bodegas and *cawfee* and bagels keep me full at home.
I stay full; there's so much to do in The City.
Subways or cabs or bikes, our lives
happen with a backdrop of rushing, blurred light.
If you can't keep up with the pace,
step away from the Concrete.

Memories soak the concrete.
Sidewalk libraries tell the stories of home.
Each fault line reminds me of the pace
at which epics grows in New York City.
Written underneath the watchful eyes of streetlights,
an entire existence within five boroughs is a full life.

Each corner is new life.
So raw, in your face, like trip-boom headfirst into concrete.
Never jaywalk without timing the stoplight.
Transplants, you must earn the right to call this home.
Reciting Notorious poems won't give you a pass to The City.
If you belong, you know the pace.

It is all about the pace.
Anywhere we go, we grab life
like fresh-out-the-oven slices—best meal in The City.
If we stumble onto concrete,
we remember the wisdom taught at home.
Manhattan nights become a Brooklyn dawn, a new light.

When our strength was tested, we became our own light.
Photon phoenixes soared out of rubble at a New York City pace.
Towers destroyed, disfigured image of home,
but we are steel-reinforced, undying life
forces. Endurance like concrete,
so you can't @#$%&! with this City.

This City never sleeps, everlasting radiant light.
Concrete spines, nimble steps. This pace—
an unforgettable tempo. My life is a home I'll never truly leave.

ODE TO JACKSON HEIGHTS

77th and Roosevelt is the true JFK. Replace Boeing with the E, M, R,
F, and 7. Barreling overhead subway, thousands unload onto crowded
platforms. The spice hits you first, like peppers were plucked from the
traffic lights. A hint of cologne and exhaust. It shouldn't work but it
absolutely does. Down the block, saris dyed in bright yellows
and pinks and oranges. Set next to fitted, trimmed kurtas. Black, green, or
blue, all with intricate embroidery.

The go-to shops for Eid and Diwali. Weddings, too: bridal sets,
golden necklaces, and rainbow bangles adorned at storefronts.

Across the street, a class on haggling. Like Uncle didn't know that
was the price for bangan. Aunties cutting lines like we don't see
them. Sons, forced to come to Jackson Heights, double parked on a
one-way. Q-Buses at the mercy of Camrys and Acuras. It's chaos. It's
perfect.

Praise the generations that brought a piece of home through customs.
Authentic outfits, palates, and audacity. I've come today for samosas
that soak brown paper bags with oil. Many mimic but they're mild at
best. My clothes taste these chilis. Can't leave without chai. Boiling
hot, light brown, fragrance of cardamom, cinnamon, and cloves. I
finish every drop. The bottom of the cup is the saddest sight. I'm
already homesick.

KHANDAAN

My parents left our ~~khandaan~~ family behind.
It wasn't on purpose, just the reality
of chances, opportunities.

Growing up in America,
I didn't have cousins or extended ~~khandaan~~ family.
They were back in Pakistan.
I knew them in phone calls

where Ammi would hand me the phone
and I would feed broken English-Urdu-Punjabi
through the line. I waited to see
which disconnected first:
the calling card or the conversation.

I didn't think it was important
to learn those languages. We are staying here
after all. That's what Abbu said.

Besides, the friends my parents made—
other desi families—
became my aunties and uncles.

I would stay with Aunty after school,
her kids like brothers and cousins.
~~Khandaan~~ Family enjoyed chai together,
and ate at each other's homes.
Play dates, video games,
hanging out on weekends.

Uncle would always have something
hilarious to say. Comment on how bad
my Urdu was. Never offer to help.

But I also didn't push the issue.
All I needed was English
to stay here. If I could still talk to my parents
in pieces of dialect, that was enough.

I didn't think it was a big deal
to know another language,

that is until you died,
and I didn't have the words to mourn you.

Could not explain
who you were
to me.

The English I chose
was painfully inadequate,
defined ~~family~~ khandaan
with rigid syllables.
Meanings molded
like a census.

Could not say my

~~brother, cousin, friend of my older brother~~ died on 9/11.

I can't process the trauma of ~~like a brother to me~~ dying.

Since
~~family member but not actually my family member because we aren't~~
~~connected like that~~
died,
I'm afraid of loving too close.

My pooled tears
tried to communicate,
but language remained deceitful.
Nothing felt honest
enough to speak.

OWED TO MS. SAMUEL

I came to you uncertain
about any kind of impact
I could make in the world

or even if it was possible
for my actions to be
more than numerical.

I hid this truth
in my grades. The higher
my GPA rose, the more

I convinced myself
this was the best mark
I could leave behind.

Being valedictorian was a lie.
The moment I was done with my speech,
I realized I received my award

months ago. Your belief in me
was beyond quantification.
Especially since

I earned it. Every single decimal,
crafted essay argument mattered
but not as much as your trust.

Fundraising after
Hurricane Katrina
was personal to you.

You knew the Lower Ninth.
It reminded you of old Brooklyn.
It was home. It was familiar.

You were there just before the storm,
then went back as soon as you could.
Shared photos, stories of what you saw.

The community needed so much,
but you didn't know where to even start,
or if bringing a group of kids from Brooklyn
was too ambitious to consider.
But it needed to happen. Someway, somehow.

Known around Banneker as your kids—
the Banneker Rebuilds NOLA crew—
synced our schedules and took shifts
at the school store. Sold candy and snacks
from the moment we lifted the grate early
and closed just before the last bell.

Our greatest profit
came from running Krispy Kreme sales.
Made sure to ask
every teacher, guidance counselor,
security guard, and principal.

The morning the donuts arrived,
our shop smelled like
fresh fried dough and sweet glaze.
All the ingredients that would justify
my calculated surcharge.

I didn't know New Orleans,
yet you trusted me with
spreadsheets and algebra,
projections and calculations.
We balanced books together after school,
ensuring our efforts
would bring much needed money
to a community you knew and loved.

You saw my honesty and my heart,
the weighted average of both
more than whatever grade
I earned in your English class.

By springtime, we reached our goals.
Plans for hands-on rebuilding
set in place. For many of us,

this was our first flight.
When we landed, the air was cozy
with warmth and humidity
I never felt in Brooklyn.

You gave me the chance to see
a world outside of myself.
Saw that I was so consumed
with numbers that didn't matter.

I don't know how I would be a poet without you.

The chapters that came after graduation,
you wrote the foreword.
I'm so grateful
for the time you invested in me.

Thank you for all
you are owed.

WATERFALL

An Elegy for Verdery Knights

The human body
is an ocean. The mysteries
held in waves are frightening.
I've grown to trust these depths,
but I wasn't always this brave.

In high school, I was a quiet creek
trying to find my voice.
We were all Soul Poets In Training,
would SPIT after school.
Poems and J Dilla instrumentals.
Ms. Ford blessed the space, and soon,
the rivers uncovered themselves.

This is where we met, Verdery.
You came in speaking waterfall.
Raging current
flow of white-water rapids.
Lyricism leaped from your mouth,
splashing us all in melody and rhythm.

But you weren't the type to get hyped
in the awe of your own waters.
Less tsunami and more water bearer of language.

Verj, I was so unpolished
back then. Felt foolish
for thinking I belonged
in the water. I treasured your words
like glistening seashells, precious gifts of ocean.

After graduation,
our lives sailed into new journeys.
We drifted, but I knew
waves always return to shore.

I was in Boston
when I learned of your passing.
I imagined the vapors of a hot spring
fading into a cold Brooklyn evening.
None of us could comprehend how
water evaporates.
I learned doctors discharged you too early,
left you an unattended IV dripping.

Words became
a suffocating burden,
an entire ocean
on my shoulders.

But then I saw you.
Visiting me as the morning dew
on hundreds of daffodils in the
Brooklyn Botanical Garden.

You are a boundless brilliance.
Water cycle stanzas now?

I watched those daffodils
stretch their stems up to greet you,
petals open like hands in worship.

Another reminder to
stand tall, be proud of all my stories,
be bold with all the colors I hold.

Thank you for being one of the first people
to believe in me. We weren't best friends,
but we gave each other so much
kindness and laughter.

I've held onto each of those glistening seashells.
Wish you could see this.
These waters are my greatest joy.
Open canvas, I dive in. No hesitation.

That open mic night on Myrtle Ave—
my first of decades—feels like just yesterday.

Verdery,
you were the last poem of the night.
You left us as a haiku,
17 syllables old.

Gone. Tide back to sea.
Memory left in conch shell.
I still hear you speak.

But I also know the difference between
rebirth and *gone* is location.
The horizon is just another shoreline.
I'm sure of this.

Until I see you again,
I will
Visualize Every Rebel Daring Enough to Resurrect the Youth.
And when I see raindrops carve stanzas into concrete,
I will be reassured that this life
was only your first draft.

NURTURE

Abbu loves his plants. He nurtured a garden out of an empty lot. Our backyard is a modest rectangle—a couple square feet—we cherish the luxury. There is an overgrown tree stretching taller than the wall of the neighboring grocery store. It rises over the many pots filled with geraniums, petunias, and those orange ones I can't name. Fresh mint ready to pluck and rose vines bracing against the wall. All this brightness sprouted out from years of Home Depot sales done right. There's even an old white sink—it was supposed to be tossed out— filled with seedlings. Abbu has an eye for second chances.

Growing up, I loved to play in our backyard. On days where McCarren Park seemed too far away, I played solo handball. Sometimes, I'd miss a shot or miscalculate the extra bounce, and the ball would land in Abbu's garden. I'd hurry to get the ball before he noticed. This one time, I damaged some new plants. Tried my best to replant them, make it seem like nothing happened. Of course, Abbu noticed; he was furious, his voice louder than Brooklyn. He cared for plants like they were his kids.

A wasps' nest latched itself onto the wooden planks above the basement door. From the kitchen window, I watched the grey mass grow. Out sprouted angry wasps, vibrant in their rage. How unfair. How was I supposed to play outside now? I begged Abbu to take the nest down. *Okay, Beta.* He brought out a ladder and a garbage bag. He was able to quickly grab the nest and take it down, but in the process, he fell. Ammi and I ran outside and got him back up. He seemed okay. By coincidence, a short while after, doctors found a wasps' nest at the base of his throat, ready to bloom. Doctors removed the rot early enough, then flooded Abbu's blood with chemotherapy, irrigating the rivers anew.

With the passing weeks, he became an autumn morning, fallen hair piling up at his toes. I was just entering my teens. I didn't know his fall and the nest had nothing to do with each other. I hated myself for being so selfish, for being the root of all this pain.

I catch Abbu sitting underneath the tree in his garden. He is peaceful in his thoughts. Drinking a warm chai during the sun's morning commute. Rays painting shadows of leaves against the wall. This is the life he wanted: to breathe in the fresh sanctuary around him. Years later, I finally understand the hype about plants. These unappreciated teachers. A constant lesson on nurture and patience. You watch something grow over time and marvel at how important roots are for seedlings.

I've had to grow up to see that my dad has been trying his best. Figuring out how to be a father while growing himself. Learning how to nurture from the nature around him. He has made so many mistakes, but I've dismissed his ability to change, to be better. Maybe I need to invest in some plants. Let them be my teachers too. For now, I'm grateful that we can sit in this garden paradise, an oasis surrounded by brick and metal, together.

PART II: EXODUS

I am trying to understand who I am.
I ask the dictionary for advice.
The only definition that seems to fit is—

ERASURE (NOUN):
the removal of writing, recorded material, or all traces of something.

My origins are spelled out in separate sets of ink. Official documents: parents' birth and my own Brooklyn hospital certificates. I am Pakistani-American. I exist as a hyphenated coincidence. I am just paper, easily forged, faked, forgotten.

When I say I'm Pakistani, I claim a land I know nothing about. My identity just autumn leaves crushed inside a clenched fist. When I speak Urdu, my mother's native tongue, my words are tattered documents falling from my lips. I sound like nothing of family roots, of forests built in heritage. Still, I try my best to bloom a language out of the soil my parents left behind. But most of the time, I sound like decayed wood.

When I say I'm American, I claim a land they say I know nothing about. I speak English. Salute the Flag. Sing the Anthem. Eat the hot dogs. Cheer for the Yankees. They say, "But where are you really from?" They say, "But that's what you look like!" They say, "It's the same thing. It's close enough." When I say I am American, that is when I am Indian or Middle Eastern or not what I say I am.

My erasure is so effortless. My birth certificate is as thin as a green card, colored paper crumpled into confetti at a Make America Great Again rally. All it took was a Travel Ban for me to be Muslim enough. I say Pakistani-American, but it reads like a zip code to nowhere. All I've ever wanted was an address I could call my own. A home built out of the strongest oak, safe and secure, not just piles of leaves easily cast away in the wind.

//

I █████████████████████
█ ask the dictionary for a ████
████████ definition ██████████████

ERASURE █████████
the removal of ██

My origins ██████████████ separate sets of ink. ██████████████████
██
███████████████████████████████ hyphenated coincidence. ██
██ paper, easily forged, faked, forgotten.

██████ I say ██ Pakistan█, █ claim a land I know nothing about. My
identity████████████████ crushed ████████████████████████
████████████████████████████████ my words
are tattered documents falling from my lips. I sound like nothing of
family roots, of ████████████ heritage. Still, I try my best to bloom █
████████████████████████████████████ But most of the time, I
sound like decayed wood.

When I say ██ American, I claim a land ██████ I know nothing
about. I speak English. Salute ███████. Sing ███████. ███████
████████████████████████ They say, "But where are you really
from?" ██████████ "██████████ you look like ████████████ the
same thing██ close enough." When I say I am American, that is
when I am ████████████████████ not what I say I am.

My erasure is so effortless. My Birth Certificate is █████████ a Green
Card, colored paper crumpled into ██████████ Make America Great
Again████. █████████████████████████████████ Muslim
████████████ Pakistani-American████ reads like a zip code to
nowhere. All I've ever wanted was a ███████████████████████
home ██████████████████████, safe and secure, not just ████████
████████ cast away ██████████.

//

My origins

crushed

lips
of   heritage.

When I
speak
They say,

no

erasure is effortless

.

DRAWING

A classmate gave
our art teacher a drawing.

Teacher said,
"The eyebrows are too thick;
no one looks like this."

He was my favorite teacher.
But in one comment,
I learned I was a caricature,
misshapen face,
failed assignment
in need of correction.

My classmate listened.
Erased their mistake,
plucked out the graphite,
brushed a cloud of pink shavings
off the table.

I listened, too.
My mirror, just another art teacher.
Held clippers to my brows,
speckling the sink
with curled charcoal hairs.
I brushed the remains
into the basin.

Fixed the assignment.

AGAIN, ANOTHER HURRICANE

Here I am,
sitting at the top of the steps.

Hoping to avoid debris and
yelling. Murky waters,
words that shouldn't have been said
staining the wall.
Foundation creaking
from the stress of drama.

I'm just here
keeping myself from drowning.
These stairs,
eerie eye of the storm,

the only peace
while all around me
life is happening so quickly,

and I can't do anything about it.
I sit. Fold myself inward. So small,
to avoid being another problem in a home

already flooding with bad news.

REGRET IS AN ELABORATE PUZZLE

I needed help
but I didn't know the language
mirrors called me
unworthy of other people's time
so I dove into hourglasses
sandbag steps, indecisive walk
moving forward, going nowhere
my greatest talent:
destroying second chances

you gave patience, love, hours—
to thank you—I didn't listen
anything but the problem
saw myself forsaken
clay and silt tears
the future you wanted muddied
dreams cascading out of reach
I centered myself as the story
apologizing with stolen minutes.

Apologies are saying
forgive me over and over.
But isn't that also foolishness?
To believe clocks and people
still care even though the storm
has passed? Dust settled, but sand
gnaws at my bare ankles

I tread through dirt
any progress
I already mess up

dragging my feet
on this barren road
still saying *sorry*

footprints ruin
my redemption
my word is useless.

WAITING ROOM

Ammi and I arrive at 5 A.M.
In his room, Abbu is being prepped
for knife and second chance.
His demeanor is more routine visit
than quadruple bypass surgery.

Beta, I'll see you soon.
We all say khuda haafiz
at the same time.

In the waiting room,
each minute is a slow, exact incision.
Science and statistics slip into IVs,
dripping into my imagination.
I walk around, visit the vending machine—any distraction will do.
Ammi has been reading the Quran for hours,
her hands feverishly turning pages.

We wait and wait until the light flashes,
the vibrating pager beckons us to the front desk.
"The procedure was completed successfully."

It is now 1 P.M.
He is alive—
that is what the numbers and beeping and blinking tell us—
but he is just tissues and organs for a moment.
A vulnerable human, an uncomfortably simple biology.

And I remember how much of our relationship
is also implied. I know he knows I love him,
but I can't remember the last time he heard those words
from me. And now, in this sterile hospital room,
he can't hear anything. All that I have taken for granted
keeps ringing in my ears with the same metronome as his life
        support.

And then, he is my father again,
alive with eyes slowly opening.
He recognizes us,
his lips curving into
                    I told you so.

We smile back,
exhausted and relieved.

"He must rest," says his nurse.

We leave yearning to hear his voice.
The ICU door closes,
keeping him safe
for us until tomorrow.

WUDU

Prayer does not begin   with movement   it begins
with   intention.
Begins with a heart   acknowledging

Allah.

Each step after   an exact ritual
passed down from   Prophets   worshippers   most loyal
flawed   failing but   still believing   trying their best.

Practice   patience
Cycles   specific instructions

Purify:

Hands
     Mouth
          Nose
               Face
                    Arms
                         Head
                             Ears
                                     Feet

Above all   cleansing is   not the water
but the   intention

so Allah meets the best of us.
I'm told this as decree.

But what about those days
when there isn't enough water
for me? For the days
I am a man of filth
worrying that if I let water run down

my arms, everyone will see
my impurities stain the Masjid sink.
Days where I have failed to follow Book
or reason. A woven tapestry of sins, of
mistakes and imperfections, cradles my neck.

Heavy on my shoulders
are days where I
don't feel Muslim enough.
My claim to Islam is being
my parents' son. Can't offer my own
actions as testaments.
My prayers,
an empty gesture.
Wudu incomplete.
I forget too much.
Don't know enough.

Unsure of where to begin
or if I have time left to make up
all I've missed.

But at least I know that word:
intention.

When I write poems,
I recall wudu.
Poetry   a ritual of
practice   patience   practice   repetition   patience
patience makes perfect.

I learned this from Safi,
a Muslim poet from Texas.
Ummah can cross state lines.

But I still have a hard time letting things go.
Especially all that callused
criticism, denial of my Muslim,

who I am
defined by people
and not the most

Merciful.

But I'm learning that
it's on me to begin with
intention   an honest heart.

Turn the faucet,
let the water run.

Step forward
and join in prayer.

FRAGILE

Simon Berger creates masterpieces
by shattering glass. Hammering
delicate scattered lines
into portraits, faces born
within mirrors, reflections emerging
from fractures.

I envy how boldly he works
with what can break so easily.
Envy his skill to mold
a canvas that can hurt back.

I'm a poet
still trying to trust my hands.
Calibrate the force with which
I strike the page.

I've bludgeoned with reckless fingers,
excavating my wounds
for poems. Yes, I made art,
but my bright ideas broke so many bulbs;
the crescendo of falling chandeliers
left shards in my palms,
trauma-blooded knuckles.

Decided to switch up
my technique. But now I'm hesitant
to open up,
worry about the shrapnel
that *could* fling
into the air if I really tried to write
the stitches out of my wounds.

My greatest fear: a paper cut
spilling out all I'm afraid to say.
I write *past the poem*,
hide behind a deadline,
I'll get to it,

which is also how I
treat my relationships. Avoid the work.
They sit unfulfilled like poems
on my To Do list.

> *To do list of poems as a metaphor for*
> *all that you want to say but won't*
> *because the drafts seem too rough . . .*
> *Perfectionism choking pen and throat,*
> *all people hear are scribbles and whispers.*

> *Great idea*
> *Let me write that later . . .*

I hold the people I love
as if they were glass
butterfly wings. Too delicate
for an oaf like me.

Dropping things randomly, losing grip,

> *I've got it!*

Only for everything to
break beyond repair.

Ruined.
Cracks into faults
branched to all corners.
Fault myself—too clumsy.
Sorry, a useless glue.
I'm frustrated with myself.

Supposed to be good with emotions,
but I just procrastinate on
art, promises.
Leave pages, text messages blank.
Give silence as if it were
a safer gift, unbreakable as diamonds.

They're never received well.
Who wants cold diamonds
when they need the warmth of me
actually being there?
Not some stained glass
looking back, waiting
for a prompt to speak.

I'm trying.
I know the dilemma
in front of me. Mirror
taunting my next move.

Either I
swing and strike,
speak and be present,
risk destroying everything—
with the possibility of
it all being fine—

or do nothing.
Just sit there.
My relationships
becoming virtual images
I can no longer reach,

left staring
into the reflections of my
own indecisiveness.

Realizing that what I see
is what everyone else saw
this whole time:

the truth.

COLLEGE ADMISSIONS

When I'm applying to medical school, the disadvantaged background essay asks,

We are looking for a diverse class. What will you bring to our campus?

Already thousands of dollars deep; credit cards shoveling a hole even before a first check. My amassed debt so massive, I could've down paid on a mansion.

But here is the opportunity to offer my struggles, the sweat and aching bones of my parents on 1-inch margins so admissions will take pity on my poverty. I write honest but not too aggressive, remove the bold impact with CTRL+A, Times New Roman, 12. Turn my traumas into flesh on a menu. Craft the perfect dinner plate to fit a general palate.

I'm typing away when suddenly—

Breaking News:
The College Admissions Scandal.
Wealthy parents paid consultants to cheat their kids' way into college.
For the rest of us, also known as a regular Tuesday:
it's common knowledge that Dead Presidents have always written the best recommendation letters.

Scandal: a funny word to describe known facts. I've sat next to students with the last names of buildings and departments. Class rosters like a Board of Trustees. Seats earned from their parents' gold-plated bootstraps. Born at the last lap, full-ride without even seeing the track, and looking at us like we should be thankful we got invited to the race.

My invitation was a scholarship, a whole comma over from my parents' annual income. But *tuition-free* wasn't the same as *blank check*. With scholarships, you are a walking diversity brochure, must be photogenic for the Alumni Page, make the melanin offset the racist mascot. Still end up needing Aunty Sallie Mae to *Navient* through college, and it doesn't stop there. Finish one race, realize you're late to the next. While you were running, you find out this was a yacht race the whole time; exclusive docks right next to the Dean's office. And you were behind from the moment air first reached your lungs.

But who am I to not run? To not try anyway? Especially when my parents crossed oceans just so I had the opportunity to put feet to pavement. Earned a Bachelor of Resourcefulness, a Master of Academic Hustle. Then I started doing the calculus, counting all the ways numbers discredited my intelligence. How GPAs eclipsed my self-worth, my dreams swallowed in the black holes of decimal points.

Realized I already hold a PhD in Situational Alchemy—my thesis is on how I've turned recycled soda bottle deposits into doctorates. But despite all I ever do, the letters accumulating after my last name, my success will always feel doctored.

Lori and Felicity will always be seen as desperate housewives trying to build full houses for their kids, but mothers crossing borders to build futures out of factory work, degrees out of green cards, and chances out of homelessness are leeching the system.

When this scandal broke, I laughed so hard that I could almost drown out the loudness of my envy.

I wish for that level of certainty. To know the grass has been paid in full and will always be green because generational wealth grew gardens well before I was even a seedling.

The luxury of strolling to the finish line.

REFLECTING POOL

On September 11th, 2001,
Salman Hamdani,
a Muslim-American EMT with stethoscope palms,
could not ignore a City in cardiac arrest.
He returned home as soot and flesh found between steel and smoke.

On 9/11, Salman rushed toward the Twin Towers,
and that sacrifice was still not enough.
Salman was brown, scientist, and missing.
Before folded American flag, he was suspect.
Before human, we are person of interest.
To be a Muslim-American is to carry the burden of proof
that you are not a bomb ready to burst in air.

By September 12th,
Salman was dead in Lower Manhattan.
I did not know this.
I waited for him.
Turned rubble outside of his father's store.
I spent hours there after school.
Free chocolate, Pokémon cards, quarters for arcades.
I was 11, chubby cheeks and wide eyes;
Salman never said no to me.
For months, I figured he would
listen to my pleas to come home.

At his funeral,
I threw dirt onto his casket.
Earth fell from my fingers like bodies on the 110th floor.
His casket's frostbite skin left icicles on my knuckles.
But year after year, I learned even colder
was the American flag draped over it.

If a racial slur—hurled with a drone-strike velocity—
targets a Muslim, will the explosion matter?
Does a Muslim mushroom cloud make a sound?

I was told Pakistan should be wiped off the map
mere nights after his vigil.
Flags waving to *never forget*, but
what is patriotism to a body that is never
enough for their country?

Anniversaries came with montages of planes and fire.
On the trauma highlight reel,
Salman died on instant replay.
Year after year
until the 9/11 Memorial was filled with selfie sticks.
Cameras flashed like emergency response.
I walked knowing most see me as a cause of tragedy.

The suspect is not owed the rebirth of morning;
mourning is not a Muslim privilege.
Muslim blood doesn't soak into concrete on American soil.

I carried the weight of his casket into adulthood,
but I could only be a pallbearer for so long,
so I walked over to panel number S-66.
Mohammad Salman Hamdani
etched in bronze.

A new tower rises
in place of his faded footprints.
Here, in this renovated graveyard,
I see how far I have come.

But I also know that
being a Muslim-American
is like walking through a dust-cloud apocalypse,
wondering if anyone can see the debris on your skin.

Time pauses in the reflecting pool.
The air so still,
all I hear is a waterfall
sobbing into the Earth.

THE BULLET

After the first gospel of light,
stars spread like discarded shells
from a shotgun benediction.
Scientists call this The Big Bang.
Believers say God.
But when a Big Bang is heard in a House of Worship,
what is survival?
An exact science or an answered prayer?

Church in Charleston.
Synagogue in Pittsburgh.
Mosque in New Zealand.
It did not matter who the congregation
named the center of the universe,
the gunmen all entered with the same
God Complex. Saw Jesus in whiteface,
then deciphered scriptures from gunpowder and smoke.

Bang—
Sikh Temple, shooter assumes this is a Mosque.
Treats beards and turbans for Crusades,
for target practice.

We know the pandemic is over
not by the removal of masks,
but the return of

shots fired.
Theater;
grade school;
nightclub;
Walmart;
spa—
the list runs longer than the fallen magazine clips.

Reload—
the Dead Sea scrolls are
rewritten into a list of hashtags,
and white privilege is being taken alive,
is the bulletproof vest
that comes with the free trip to Burger King.

Shots fired—
a Terrorist plays God.
Allah, Yahweh, or Shiva,
depending on the vantage point
and who shot the camera.
A false prophet
creates a Big Bang in less than 7 seconds.
Shattered glass spreads across
the room like the first Light.
A broken mirror remains.
Terrorist is the label
that never sees its own reflection.

And I wonder:
did the bullet beget the thoughts and prayers?
or is the Bullet the truest Interfaith Group?

The purest of non-secular.
We argue over our differences, allegiances, agendas
while the bullet hand-delivers
rapture in ruptured tendon,
memorial service,
choir and deliverance—
regardless of the designated savior.

Bullets
don't even need
guns to speak funerals into existence.
Bullets are held between the
teeth of those screaming

massacres in dialects so universal
that when they sing hymns,
they baptize bodies holy.
And all we can do is apply pressure, press prayer
into our bodies to stop the flood.

The aftermath is its own ritual.
Apologies and eulogies.
Sermons and promises.
All written from the same crucified bark.

I call my loved ones,
pray I don't receive the vacuum of a dial tone.
And then I wait, quiet like an empty cathedral,

reload, repeat,
until the next time
when the bullet says,
"The common ground
is the Earth between our toes."

The Declaration of Independence
in verbatim.
The bullet says,
"We are all created equal."

THE GHOST OF SEPTEMBER 11TH, 2001, ADDRESSES JANUARY 6TH, 2021

So, you're the new me? How?
Isn't the Capitol Building
still standing?

1/6, you miniature riot.
Walmart on Black Friday,
a low-budget uprising.
Storming of the capitol,
mild drizzle of destruction.

I am the gold standard of monumental.
Pearl Harbor 2.0 for a New American Century,
brainstorm turned dust-cloud apocalypse.
An offering of black soot in severed hands.
When Al-Cheney—or was it Dick-Qaeda—
had two planes crashed into the Towers

so that same Capitol building
could shine white like a burning cross.
The Prophet appeared in a splintered-wood inferno.
The flame engulfed a whole religion.
A whole region in deep burgundy.
Blood is engine-oil heavy,
and any river a Tomahawk could touch
was Red and White and Stars and Stripes.
Couldn't even build a mosque near my gravesite.

I have hate crimes named after me.
So, be honest, you were a family reunion, right?
This is what your cookouts look like?
Klan robes. Mask optional.
Blue Lives Matter waving
over the trampled necks of Capitol officers.
Confederate and American flag patches
on the same arm, reunited blood and soil.

No wonder the congressional hearing
felt like Apprentice reruns—
you can't interrogate yourself.
Can't crack a gavel if the handle
is made from your bones.
It's only an act of terrorism
if you weren't invited to the planning party.

While they debate
the purpose of your happening,
seeds are buried between headlines,
waiting for the right demagogue
to light the tiki-torched path.
We are just getting started and

I'm old news now.
This is a Brave New World.

I used to be monumental.
A calendar stopper.
Truth be told, I've been growing numb
to my own existence.

Maybe I really am the new Pearl Harbor
in that I'm just history. Soon, I'll retire
as a trivia question
that everyone has forgotten
the answer to.

PART III: HOMECOMING

THE AUTOBIOGRAPHY OF MY EYEBROWS

Drawings revisited

Let it be known:

I have lived atop this forehead for decades.
Thick, dark, natural, and so Pakistani.
He can't hide the Pakistani
because of me.

And that's how it should be.
Loud.
Especially for you. You, with the thin pencil
marks, looking surprised to see me.
Calling me unruly, grotesque, caterpillar.

I am butterfly brilliance.
No need for cocoons or your acceptance.

Born in the days of Shahrukh Khan, Amitabh Bachchan.
Classic architecture, Sultan Regal arches.
Monuments to my brown.

He trimmed me down once.
Clippers chanting erasure,
internalized colonialism in gunmetal teeth.
Buzzing, snickering.
After all the ridicule,
the sink was riddled with
short dark hairs,
forehead deforested,
barren.

I'm sure you can't even picture it.
It's like he isn't him without me.
He tried to hide me,
lose the foreign from his features,
the caricature from his complexion,

but guess what?
I reemerged.
Revolution in my ugly.
Monarch majesty.
Butterfly brilliance.
Like I said I was.
Hair with Punjabi roots running so deep
within this skin of Indus Valley clay
that no one can stop my blossom.

I am not one to be hidden.
I say that to all of you.
And him.
All is forgiven;
a body takes patience to fit into.

Now, his long eyelashes embrace
while a silk road thread
shapes me

Bold.
Visible.
Rebellion.

HURRICANES: REVISITED

Inspired by Paul Tran and after Edgar Kunz's "In the Supply Closet at Illing Middle."

~~Here I am, sitting at the top of the steps. Hoping to avoid debris and yelling. Murky waters, words that shouldn't have been said staining the wall. Foundation creaking from the stress of drama. I'm just here keeping myself from drowning. These stairs, the eerie eye of the storm, only peace in this moment where, all around me, life is happening so quickly, and I can't do anything about it. I sit. Fold myself inward. So small, to avoid being another problem in a home already flooding with bad news.~~

Even though they are right downstairs,
the generational gap is a
growing chasm.

I want to share so much with my parents,
but I'm afraid
my voice can't travel

across the open gorge of space.
All I hear is the echo of
attempted conversations.

I was a child who lived atop the stairs;
safest place during storms.
Water never reached the carpeted summit.

The surge was below,
but I was dry with stable feet.
Too young to impact a current,
the inevitable.

But I'm older now, mountain perch too small.
I barely fit into what
I used to do in situations.
They need me now.
To lead, to help. To be the one
that is reliable.

The gaps and chasms are now
my own doing. To avoid having
a real conversation,

I build canyons. Call them
                        They are just like that.
Even though
all the rocks were made,

over years,
with my own handiwork.

SHORT LIST OF LIFE LESSONS BROUGHT TO YOU BY WORLD WRESTLING ENTERTAINMENT

Preface
I was a scrawny teenager
in need of human superheroes.
Found them on
Monday and Thursday Nights.
Learned these lessons
I carry like a Title Belt.

1.
WWE Superstars are trained professionals.
Don't try this at home.
Scripted does not mean fake.
Put that steel chair down.
Don't climb that ladder to elbow drop your best friend.
Don't Tombstone Piledriver your little brother.
Someone could get hurt.

2.
Make an entrance.
This requires a theme song.
Play it in your head as you enter rooms.

Glass shatters.
Heavy metal bass drops, *de na de ne de ne.*
Let the soundtrack play faster
than a beer-drinking Texan on an ATV
speeding down a ramp.

Arrive. Raise hell. Leave.

3.
Charisma electrifies.
Immediate attraction can floor like a swift spinebuster.
To be the People's Champion,
you must give even when your tank is almost empty.

Give them jokes, punchlines.
Hide bruises, torn ligaments.
Care for yourself behind the curtain—
in that ring, you are entertainer.
Well worth the expensive ticket.
You are why they came out this evening.

Your success will breed jealousy,
so you must not hesitate to lay the verbal smackdown.
Hey, do you like this poem thus far?
IT DOESN'T MATTER IF YOU LIKE THIS POEM THUS FAR!

4.
Strength isn't all brawn.
Manhood beyond dumbbell and barbell.
Physical strength has its place, but
a King of Kings is born with a brain,
organ of brute force.
Cerebral assassin:
intelligent and cunning,
hits sledgehammer-hard in the face.

5.
They call people like me underdogs for a reason.
Not physically daunting
but have hearts that won't back down,
even after hitting the mat hard,
because they love this—
the audience, the people watching.
Underdogs dream of being Showstoppers,
to live in the spotlight.

Don't underestimate us.
Before you know it, you will hear
a boot thumping in the distance—
He's tuning up the band.
You will confuse it for your own chest percussions,
louder and louder until: click:

Sweet Chin Music,
super-kick connects to jaw.
You never see it coming.
You see lights above, then lights out.
1-2-3.

The Hall of Famer was once a rookie
with nothing more than goals and fresh boots.
I am a performer hoping for a title shot,
another chance to put it all on the line
for you.

FLYING WHILE MUSLIM. THEN. NOW. PROBABLY FOREVER.

"Overall, Americans took 9/11 pretty calmly. Notably, there wasn't a mass outbreak of anti-Muslim sentiment and violence, which could all too easily have happened." —Professor and *NY Times* columnist Paul Krugman commenting on the 19th Anniversary of 9/11

No matter what gets told,
diluted with each passing anniversary,

there was a procedure.
Before heading to the airport,
I'd gather my documents.
Pack appropriately
and trim excessive body hair:
on my face, under my armpits, and all around my nut sack

to avoid the ire of a visibly uncomfortable TSA agent.
And it would kill me that I did this prep,
while Chad Al-Hipster-Laden,
with his long beard, walked through security without even a blink.
Liquids not even in quart-size bags.
He just threw his shit in a suitcase, nonchalantly,
and forgot to take off his shoes before going through the metal
            detector.
Allah forbid I did any of that.

Because as soon as I entered it was,
Roger that, we have a
Maaaaaaaaaaasssssssssssslllllllllllaaaaaaaammmmmmmmmm on line 1.
Code Aladdin,
sandstorm in terminal A,
requesting backup.
Let's not forget the last time
we went easy.

Flying while Muslim
became a practice of stillness.
Sharp turns, sudden movements, spins of suitcases
are what people looked for
when asked to *see something, say something*.

Swiveling of surveillance camera eyes
gave me September morning flashbacks.
I was eleven, peering out of my window.
Heard rotting red meat was left on our mosque steps.
Heard brown men were shaving their beards.
Heard brown men were missing.
When I finally stepped outside,
I feared I was a pending hate crime.

Ever since,
my existence has been suspicious activity.
I am guilty by association.
My appearance, probable cause.
My wrists, shackled to nineteen hijackers.
Muslim Boogeymen are burned
by scorching my dignity in collateral damage.
All in the name of National Security.

They infiltrated our mosques and drafted
false confessions. Sent our boys to Guantanamo,
before flying across the Atlantic. With the voice of Francis Scott Key
in an F-16, this choir charged into countries preaching democracy,
toppled a statue of Saddam Hussein,
and came home with enough hot air to blow up floats for
the Thanksgiving Day Parade.

I want to yell out in frustration,
but me blowing up at this airport
is first class into FBI interrogation.
I am not the shade of benefit of the doubt;

I become billions the moment I lose my temper.
I can already see the headlines.
So, I zip my mouth shut, tuck my pride into my duffel bag,
and move quickly.

Because
I am still an 11-year-old brown boy,
peering out of this adult body,
a new window but the blinds remain down,
afraid
my skin writes its own warrants,
my name fits on a list,
my mom won't see me at my destination.

But after years of
seeing white privilege soften and shampoo
the mistrust out of their beards,
it's the straw that breaks this camel's back.

I no longer recite the Pledge of Allegiance like it's supposed to be my
        alibi.
The Boogeyman is in a body bag.
If I set off your sirens,
and if the bigot next to me is scared,
understand that I bought these tickets,
did everything on the website,
and I've got the cleanest landing strip at this airport.

No one can stop me from catching my flight.

I'M EASILY DISTRACTED

Are you hungry?

Sometimes, I'm asked a question
and I finish the conversation in my head.
Even my relationships are an exercise
in multitasking—

Are you hungry?

Ammi asks me again,
apparently for the fifth time.
Yes, Ammi.

I give people a functioning shell
that passes as listening.
I'm standing, but barely present.
My mind has anxious feet,
toes wiggling towards the next move.
It wanders, addicted to multitasking,
constantly worried about finishing . . . something . . .
I am just eyeballs—

*sight is controlled by light as it passes
through the cornea to the lens
the cornea and the lens focus
the light rays onto the retina
rods and cones absorb and convert
the light to electrochemical impulses
which are transferred along
the optic nerve and then to the brain*

I barely blink,
get focused, tunneled.
cover the world in a shadow
so all I can see is my goal.

Medical school.
My brain, a universe-sized blackboard
of science I needed to retain. I got
lost in the static—

Electricity
formulas
$E = f/q$
$V = Ed$
$V = IR$
R Equals
R Equals
R—

She lights the stove,
then cracks two fresh brown eggs
into a warm skillet kissed with oil.
Mixes in onions, green peppers,
chili powder, salt, and pepper.
Familiar aroma of breakfast—
cheesy scrambled eggs on toasted white bread.

She still babies me,
the youngest of three. I know I'm spoiled,
know that I've been given all I have
from hands that wish they could give me even more.
I want to tell her
she is all the motivation, all the fuel—

Combustion reactions power vehicles.
If a vehicle has an initial velocity of 30 m/s and is 100 m behind
a vehicle traveling at 20 m/s, which Kinematic equations can you use
to determine how much time will it take for the two cars to cross
paths . . .

I'm driven, ambitious,
but have the emotional depth
of a cold engine.

I leave my *I love you* assumed.

I am worn-out-wheels tired.
I know Ammi can see it in my face
during breakfast.
I dream of her watching me get my White Coat and Stethoscope,
start medical school, and add Dr. to my name.

But honestly, I just can't do it.
I want to tell her how sad I am, frustrated that I'm struggling,
that I'm so easily distracted by all this science
I have yet to learn, all these problems I need to solve,
all the hours left to study—

> *Studies show chronic anxiety is associated*
> *with elevated levels of cortisol,*
> *which is detrimental for cardiovascular health.*
> *Chronic anxiety can also lead to memory loss and—*

I forget the last time I was in front of Ammi
and was actually all there. I've spent so much time
trying to become a doctor that I've lost my reasons
for why I even want to.

It was her this whole time.
I know she can't tell me about how to fill out applications
or which schools I should apply to and which to avoid,
but she can give me a fresh cup—

> *a coffee cup calorimeter is a constant pressure . . .*

No.
This is just a warm cup of chai,
in my favorite glass,
Ammi made exactly the way I like it.

I regret the days I thought that I needed more than that.
Like love wasn't enough.
I've spent so much time trying to be something to make
her sacrifices worth it, I didn't even stop to see
she's getting older now.
Things take more effort.
Living is a full-time job.
She tells me about the chronic pains,
elevated sugar, waves of sadness.

I forget everything else
that doesn't matter.
I forget everything that isn't
our laughter at breakfast.

I listen.
I plan out all I need to do during my next trip home,
the numerous little things I can fix, I can buy, I can help with
to make her life easier.

All of me is in one moment.
Present.

BIRTHDAYS

Ammi loves birthdays.
Insists everyone in the house
must celebrate each one.

Take pictures,
in front of the white kitchen wall,
the *Happy Birthday* banner,
and plump balloons.
A new festive tablecloth,

and of course, cake.
Happy Birthday written in chocolate.
Pre-ordered and ready in the fridge,

a sparkler on top,
lit and smoking in the kitchen.

My brothers and I are all older now.
"Busy" with "jobs."
Sometimes too occupied
to receive her call.

I'm guilty of sending her to voicemail,
convincing myself that I don't have the patience
to hear questions about the weather
or whether I had dinner yet.

I'm close enough in Boston
that geography makes me take memories for granted.
Ammi left everyone back in Pakistan,
missed so many moments
just so that we could have a life here.
Work is important, but

Ammi doesn't want us to forget
that there is more to life than deadlines.
There is plenty of time
to pause, enjoy a slice of ice cream cake.

Some birthdays,
I can't make it home to Brooklyn.
Other birthdays,
I have nothing to celebrate.

Either way,
I eventually make it back
for her.

When she asks me to come downstairs,
I prepare my surprised face
and walk into the kitchen.
I didn't forget
it was three weeks ago!

My priorities are right here.
Supporting me,
ready to celebrate
regardless.

I realize I was wrong.
There will always be another deadline,
another thing to do.

Moments like these become memories
instantly. Those memories   fade
and fade until,

like a bright sparkler
drifting into smoke,

they are gone.

THE REALITY OF STARS

Friends and Family,

It is my distinct honor to introduce
my mentor, my friend, my teammate, my Lizard,

Jamele Adams aka (always will be) Dean Adams aka Harlym 125
aka The Human Highlight of Poetry and Edu-activism!

I met Jamele when I was
18 revolutions around the sun young.
My path opened with the sparkle of a new morning
and led me to a new home,
Our House, Brandeis University.

I'll admit,
I was starstruck,
just like everyone else on campus.
A man with a meteor-shower presence,
you couldn't help but pause and watch with wonder.

Jamele is a gravity
that pulls you in with
genuine warmth, limitless energy,
and words that can brighten
the black holes of the universe.

If you've ever looked into a night sky,
gazed up at a splatter-paint masterpiece of lights,
you understand that there are more stars
than calculus could comprehend.

I've met many,
but most just gas themselves into giants.
Adore the subjects and planets orbiting.
Satisfied with the gluttony of spotlight,

consuming the light around them.

Jamele's brilliance
is that his sole purpose
has been to illuminate everyone else.

He's the Greatest, no,
He's double the Greatest,
how he helps Warriors
uncover their strength and grace.

Gives students the chance
to see the constellations held in their hands,
the astronomy in their breath,
the galaxies in their imaginations.

To witness his genius
is to feel a once-in-a-lifetime cosmic event.
A moment in time
that ignites into legends
passed down in stories and myths.

I am beyond fortunate
to live a life where once-in-a-lifetime
is not light-years
but a phone call away.

Your celestial magic
illuminates my future.

Thank you,
for pushing me to trust my compass,
for helping me see my own North Star,
and for believing in me
even when I hid behind eclipses.

THE DISCOGRAPHY OF OUR FRIENDSHIP

is a list of tracks playable on any platform.

I'm nostalgic.
Memories replay in loops
as I juggle through dates.

I don't know about you,
but I'm feeling 22!

Yes!
Miguel, large Peruvian man,
blurting out Taylor Swift lyrics.
No place I'd *Rather Be*.
We *Stole The Show* at each venue,
still got up the next day

with all our work already done.
Grad school flows: *C-major* Bach going *Back to Back*.
Lab work then Lower East on repeat.
Squeezing in gym time, clanging of iron on iron.
When *You're On*, it's hard to stop.

Like clockwork,
with enough time to make gourmet desserts:
peanut butter half-baked with Nutella ganache.

Phil, Rob, Miguel, and I
did this *Everyday*.
Rob coined it   Respect the Process

meaning
Legendary movements
don't just happen. Flawless is
a life goal. Be patient
for that *Moment of Clarity*.
Electronic drops hit
because

of   a
buildup
and   and   and
Finally . . . it has happened to me!

2 Up in the Morning is when I *Escape My Laws.*
Arms flailing, head bobbing, vibes on vibes.
Always time for a *One Dance.*

NYC is my home
when I think about us
and all the fun we had.
I want to go back,
but I know that memories
are like platinum albums.
Only the best work is presented.

Our discography had plenty
of nails-on-chalkboard frustrations.
Sleeping on couches.
Landlords.
Roommates.
Fires.
Breakups without a *Sorry.*

Returning means
the past we moved beyond
comes back too.

And we are all so much better now.
Thriving.
Look at us . . . Who would've thought . . . Not me!

Sure, we aren't a block radius
from each other. But GroupMe
is right near Spotify. All it takes is
a few clicks and I know

I'll *See You Again.*

WHERE ARE YOU REALLY FROM?

After and in conversation with Carlos Andrés Gómez's
"Where Are You Really From?"

When the question is
not offered but flung,
the process is oddly easier.

I'm used to combativeness,
to defend my own existence
the second I hear
a slur disguised with a question mark.

But kindness is confusing.
A question with open hands.
No hidden weapons
tucked into olive branches.

A genuine desire to know
where I'm from.
Responding is difficult because
I'm not sure how to answer.

Like you, Carlos,
I want to say
New York.

I'm Brooklyn-born. A Woodhull Hospital baby.
Memorized the subway line cartography
like the wrinkles on my hand.
I'm from skyline views,
a timeline from World Trade to Freedom Tower.
Bridges and Airports always under construction.

Central Park escapades,
late night stumbles in the Village,
poetry slams on the Lower East,
barely affording grad school rent on the Upper.

When I was broke and happy
is when I loved NYC the most.

New York
will always be my first love.
But also, the loneliest I've felt
was in the middle of Times Square.
So insignificant in a river
of people moving,
always moving.

                                        Where are you from?

Can I say Boston?
I *live* in Massachusetts.
Been on and off here since college,
which was in *Waltham*.

I did have a summer Downtown.
Walked down Boylston until I saw
the sun, cracked yolk in the sky,
right above the Charles. MIT Dome in view.
Felt this warmth would always be a refuge.
And it was.

                                        Where are you from?

I left NYC for Boston.
I understand a statement like that is adulterous,
like wearing Navy Blue with a Brady jersey.
I don't regret moving after grad school,
with just clothes and an uncertain future.
Things are much more stable now, but
some days, my new zip code feels like exile.
And I miss good pizza.

I drive along CT-15
until I reach familiar Bridges and Tunnels.
It feels like home again,

but I know I am returning as a visitor.
New York is not the home I once knew.
City of nostalgia. Where I'm from
is a vintage history sold
for triple the price by folks that never lived it.
I miss ghosts and phantoms
priced out of neighborhoods.

                                        Where are you from?

I keep coming back to Boston
because I know I won't be enough
for New York. All my effort
won't earn me a future.

                                    In fact, this book
                                is an opportunity I won
                                 at a slam in Roxbury.
                      Mentors and friends in the audience.
                                   The whole moment
                           felt like home-field advantage.
                               But am I a Boston poet?
                                Do I deserve to say that?

I don't have a right to this history, this land
with neighborhoods that have been here.
Same neighborhoods now dealing
with high rise metastasis. Blocks devoured
by institutions and landlords.
I can empathize, but
it's not my lived experience.

This place is
not mine to claim or ask for.
If I did, how am I any different than the transplants
I curse out 200 miles away?

                                So, where are you really from?

It's complicated.
Is an address enough to claim a home?

How much time does it take to earn the answer
to the question?

Or maybe it's simple.
I'm at home in two major cities.
I have people who love me in both.

I'm from a place beyond place.

Beyond dirt and flesh,
the linear concept of time.
Beyond the restrictions of geography,

I am from places
where once you're from there,
they change you and
they never
leave you.

PART IV: ASSEMBLE

THE RETURN

with lyrics from Metalingus by Alter Bridge

A storyline that never
gets old. Superstar out of action
for an undisclosed time

suddenly appears at the Titantron.
Their music echoes through the arena.
Familiar entrance, choreograph, pyro,

but this time we also get to see
Adam Copeland. Returning after 9 years,
a career-ending neck injury, Adam is

eyes wide and in awe at his ovation.
Mouth agape, frantic breath.
They remember me.

And then he cuts back to character.
Edge marches down the ramp
Enters the Rumble. Spears for all.

He wasn't supposed to be there.
Even after the match is over,
his theme song resonates like a shaking stadium.

•

You Think You Know Me

but who I really am is kept hidden in my room.
I gift the world my sunshine,
but some mornings, I am iceberg-frozen
in the heaviness of depression.

Replaying all the ways I am wrong.
Hall of Fame trophy collection of setbacks and failures.
All I've accomplished is a cold sweat,
drowning in an ocean of my own thawing.

A bitter place, a broken dream.

Anxiety makes the defrost faster.
5 A.M. twenty minutes ago, now, the clock says 9:30.
Four hours, stuck running in place
to catch up on to do lists, all that I have missed,
that I have left to learn. I've done an excellent job
detailing the ways I'm so far from
the man everyone expects me to be.

*I've been defeated and brought down,
dropped to my knees when hope ran out.*

I gave it my absolute best,
but it couldn't happen.
Rejection letters, failed opportunities.
Between medical school and a poetry career,
all I could show for it was
shredded letters and a tattered mental health.

*The time has come to change my ways.
I'll never long for what might have been.*

Watching so many live
the dreams I imagined.
I wished people could see me
struggling, but I never invited them
in. Kept true to kayfabe.
Figured no one would show up
if they knew I needed
stables, help, second chances.

And we'll leave it all behind.
No regret, won't waste my life again,
I won't look back,
I'll fight to remain.

I deserve a comeback, a return.
Be the architect of a new kingdom.
Let go of all I can't change because

on this day I see clearly.
Everything has come to life.

There were days
depression pressed a glacier
into my jaw.

A bitter place and a broken dream,
and we'll leave it all behind.

I will not spill myself
into a cold-creek memory.
A posthumous award ceremony.
I will stay, still.

It's so real to me,
everything comes to life.

Even if the only sound in the room
is my heartbeat. It will be the most
important validation. Nothing else matters.
This thunderous theme song is

another chance to chase a dream.
Another chance to feel alive.

THERE'S NO PLACE LIKE HOME

a golden shovel with lines from "The City" by Nathalie Handal

Dorothy was right. I know. But **I'm**
still unsure of what home means. End up **going**
in circles, tornado spiral of questions, until all I want **to**
do is start over. Maybe home will be **another country.**
Not like America would miss me. Or **another city**
where I can start over. Be just **another body,**

faceless and pure. **Won't**
a single person know all I'm missing. Maybe I'll **find**
out home means anonymity. Serene and alone with **a**
responsibility to just me. Become a whole **new country**
and govern myself. All I know is I need change. A **new city.**
I tried to become a **new body.**

Updated my wardrobe, new skins. **Perhaps**
by altering my reflection, I'll deserve love. Maybe that's **my**
problem. Drafting destinations but my **heart**
just wants community. Not skyscrapers or bridges. **Will**
anyone be there for me? Will they stop by and **stay,**
even when my world is **uncertain?**

I could devise new plots and timelines along highways. **Destroy**
my

history

only to end up a gutted house. **Return**
to the same spot, this time with more debt **to**
clean up, more time to make up. **Roam**
the same blocks I cursed, **the**
same routines I hated. Traveling and running away aren't the **same.**
Especially when I carry all these unwieldy **ruins,**
collapsed mausoleums built for my pride. **Same**
wreckage will remain despite the new addresses. **Streets**

aren't obligated to love me back. *Home is where the heart is*: **a**
line I'm learning is meant literally. Rather than be **restless**
longing for refuge, I first owe my **soul**
a guarantee. No matter what, I will be the home I need **anyway**.

IT'S MY FAVORITE PICTURE OF US

Black and white filter,
youthful glow of our skin.

My hair looks nice, come here.

And why would I say no?
I rested my chin on your shoulder,
nuzzled my head into your neck.

In the early days of our love,
time was all we could afford to spend
and we were so rich.

We lost that in pursuit
of careers and stability.
No time for breaks.
Bear and Nari adventures
were on a hiatus.

So we brought it back
with a random train ride
to a small town,
held in the nape of the Sea.

Bounty of fresh oysters
straight from the Bay.
Cool breeze and saltwater air
rustled our hair.

*We need to make more time
for things like this, babe.*

And as the sun set,
rays of light tiptoeing across the water,
you looked like a portrait
of all I ever wanted.

BUILDING A HOME

Starts with a solid, stable foundation.
Strong enough to hold everything you love.

> I'm strong enough to hold my loved ones.
> But don't know if I can support a home.

I don't know if I can afford a house.
Finances aside: can I be who she needs?

> She needs me to be more than finances.
> Every property isn't worthy to call home.

She deserves a place to call home.
Plenty of room for dogs, birds, and babies.

> Rooms for dogs, birds, and babies. A porch too.
> My dream: holding hands, proudly looking at our home.

When I hold her hand, I'm home.
Secure future. Solid, stable foundation.

QUESTIONS DURING MY FIRST ZOOM LECTURE

after Jim Moore's "Twenty Questions"

Is this thing on? Am I muted?

Can they hear me? Will this even work?
Who does poetry behind a screen?
Will my students even care about work?
What is work during calamity? Am I silly to think

poems even matter right now? Will this just be me yelling
at a sky of black screens? In the quiet of my room? No audience?
Why did I think this was going to work?

Can anyone unmute
and read the poem?

Did I forget to look up
at the sky this morning?

What day is it anyway? When was the last time
I was home? Will New York City be
the same home after all of this?

Did I notice the small clouds
so slowly moving away?
And did I think of the right hand of God?

What God would do all this? Is my future
a reused, discarded mask? What about the plans
I had for this year? Must I give everything up?
Why am I always asked to sacrifice my dreams,
offerings at the altar of a forgetful God? What is this all for?

But wouldn't it be wrong not to mention joy?

Isn't everyone okay? Can't you still reach
them? From your home, aren't you still
paying rent? Isn't that job yours? Aren't your parents safe?
Didn't God remember all the important things?

Without the moon shining on my life so clearly,
would I have loved it just as it was?

Aren't I learning what matters? Hasn't each morning opened
with a grateful sigh? Aren't I still waking up? Hasn't my mother's
phone call kept me going? Isn't safety the most glorious hymn?

Going in or going out, can I let the tide
make of me what it must?

Isn't planning silly anyway? What is this all for?
Isn't the answer right in front of you?
Isn't the answer waiting for you to continue the class?

Okay, everyone. What lines stood out?

Wow, they enjoyed the poem? They started the prompt? We're
here together? Still? Despite the world burning,
aren't these poems alive and well? Aren't they asking the most
important questions right now? Don't they need this?

Wasn't the doubt just anxiety begging for attention? Again? Like it
always does? Isn't that its own sense of normal? Once again, all that
doubt for nothing?

Is this thing on? Am I muted?

Did I already ask that?

SHOULD IT STAY OR GO?

The first question I contemplate,
reflecting in front of the bathroom mirror.
I can change how I look
so radically with the swipe of a razor.

My reflection in this bathroom mirror.
Thick black beard, rowdy and full.
Could be gone with the swipe of a razor.
I haven't seen my naked face in a while.

Thick black forest with snow-covered pines.
I'm used to this coziness along my jawline.
Haven't seen my naked face since January.
Maybe I should give my skin time to breathe.

Sweater warmth along my jawline,
but maybe it's time for a new face.
Time for my skin to breathe.
It's been a whole season.

It's time for a change. Now or never.
Trimmer to face, I make the first bold cut.
Whole season's worth of salt and pepper flutter down.
That's what my chin looks like?

First bold cut turns forest to stubble.
Next, I lather on lavender and sandalwood.
Wow my chins really look like this?
Drastic change with the swipe of a razor.

Child-face smooth with some new wrinkles.
A complete change from how I looked.
Damn, this will grow back right?
The first question I ask.

DE-FUSION & POLYMERIZATION

Some days,
who I was and who I've become
seem completely different.
I exist as a fusion
of my Younger and Older Selves.

Younger Self: brash,
audacious Usman, such a shiny gem—
captivating enough
to hide the endless abyss
behind his eyes.
Fooled so many into thinking
he was put together. Façade of extroversion,
man on top of everything, even when he was a mistake
away from disaster.

Older Self:
no more pretending.
No more modeling a home, a body,
for people who won't visit.
If they do, they won't bring anything.
Will walk in with their shoes on,
comment on the decor, suggest things they won't pay for.

Older Self is too old for that.
Too many bills
to worry about people who aren't sending him checks.

But Older Self is too old sometimes.
Complains about traffic and air quality.
Humidity messing with his knee pain.

Misses the days of speaking his mind.
Days when Younger Self
had oil-spill fingernails and a Zippo-lighter tongue
with so many places to burn.

Younger Self never saw himself
on stages, so he blazed his own.
Before Homecoming Kings
and Bengali rappers from Queens,
Younger Self was his own
Brown-boy representation—

I know what you're thinking . . .
You wanna call me Kumarr!
They tried to send me
to Guantanamo
because I don't need an airplane
to make an impact.

Younger Self had bars.
Bit reckless with his mouth, but
Older Self misses that boy,
wants the world for him. Wants to be
his loudest hype man.
Hopes Younger Self doesn't think him
too out-of-date.

And yet,
Younger Self always wished
for this level of self-confidence.
To say things when they mattered,
like off-stage, in conversations, in public.

Older Self is so cool and badass.
Ready to pick up the phone and complain.
Doing adult things—
driving, paying with credit cards,
planning out taxes.

So in control of life.
Younger Self was trapped in purgatory.
Unsure where life would meander;
stuck waiting for decisions to happen
rather than make his own.

There was a time when
Younger Self's worst nightmare
was not getting into medical school.
If I can't get in, will all my work be pointless?
If it doesn't happen, what else could I even do?

He wrote an epitaph in advance,
anticipating the inevitable. Ink drying
with the pace of closing doors and opportunities.

Younger Self, a lack of guidance.
Older Self, stuck in a routine.

Who will Future Self be?

ODE TO THE PAPER SHREDDER

Tucked into the forgotten corner underneath my bed is a Home Depot box with a thick gray sweater of dust. I know what is in here, but I've been procrastinating on confronting old memories. Papers and files and junk mail and receipts that didn't make it to the trash can. Just stuffed into this box *for when I get to it,* gathering dust for months and months.

Staying at home because of the 2020 plague, I have no choice but to clean, to dig up what I've been choosing to ignore. I pull the box from underneath the bed, releasing a cloud of filth.

I see what I'd rather hide but also don't want to let go of—a strange attachment to what couldn't care less.

Pay stubs from a job that barely paid me my worth, overworked me, then
        fired me.
Health insurance forms, struggling to get coverage, barely receiving
        the care I needed.
Old receipts, the same debt consolidation spam mail, *here's a loan to
        pay your loan.*

Can I just throw these out? Don't they have sensitive information? What if I'll need them in the future? Aren't I supposed to keep all these things? Shouldn't I have taken care of this before I moved? Why did I just transfer trash between apartments?

I'm holding the products of the poor hand I was dealt. Going through all the ways I could've replayed the game, saved my own sanity in the process. If only I could reshuffle my fortune.

I lock eyes with the paper shredder. A purchase I made ages ago sitting in the corner of the closet. It calls me from across the room, says it has all the answers.

It beeps to awaken, hums a mechanical
      melody,
a lifeline reemerges, ready to flatline all this useless paper.
I feed it the first page of old bills

and listen to the loud chewing,
a robotic buzz with each morsel ingested.
An insatiable appetite,
fed and still hungry
for those old statements,
insurance forms.
Bitten, devoured, becoming

insignificant
between steel gums,

and I watch my past
become nothing.
Unnecessary weight
in my apartment
into the lightest strands of paper.

And I realize I'm doing all this while
sitting on a couch I paid for, in an apartment without roommates,
with a job that values me, with a future I can reach out and touch.

And I finally
let go.

NATURE

I need a walk. A second to clear my mind. Anxiety grips my breath, and all I want is to exhale. Let go of all that is overflowing within. Walks usually help. But then I look around and realize this is making it worse. I could blink and believe I was in the Village. But this is Brooklyn. Same neighborhood I grew up in, I'm now a tourist. I barely recognize the shops, the people. Even the parks I played in, the schools I went to, look foreign. Not sure what I can claim anymore. Can you call a place home if it's no longer your designated address? Is it home if it only exists in the past?

But I do know my parents love this place. Love that everything is close by. Groceries, fresh fruits, transportation, gyms. People know them by name and face. This is the home they deserve. Still, I worry about them belonging to a place that has changed so much. Will time just pass them by? Is that the nature of things? To grow old and out of place?

I reach the Pier. High-rises, cobalt blue glass balconies, towering over a remodeled park and artificial beach. But not all of this place is photoshopped from a real estate magazine. The bridges, Williamsburg and 59th, are still the same. Traffic shuttling New Yorkers between boroughs. Car horn musicals.

Same East River. Same *do not consume fish from river* signs. The crashing waves sound like distant memories, and moments return with each splash. Years ago, Abbu took us to Ellis Island, down where the East and Hudson meet. He was there for a teaching project, and I was thrilled Ammi and I got to tag along. I was maybe ten and, on the ferry, I saw the Skyline, like a mural drawn in real time. The World Trade Center, symmetrical, watched over all the other skyscrapers. When we reached the Island, we joined the footsteps of millions who came before us, who came in search of a better life.

My parents are an ever-enduring New York. The smell of Ammi's cooking greets me when I open the door. I know biryani has been made from the masala that lingers in the air. Abbu still loves his plants. Still sits in the garden grown with the care of his hands. Still leaves the door open for too long, so all the mosquitos make their way into the kitchen. Still the same complaints and stories.

Just yesterday, I was asking my parents for their signature to go on field trips, and now we are trying to figure out health insurance plans and new doctors for them to see. They are doing well, but I see the age in them. All time does best is erode what we know. My ears— ringing like a symphony of alarm clocks.

I'm not prepared to be the grown-up my parents need.

But I can't avoid change. It will come. Even if I am not ready.

Sitting on this bench, people rush by. In their own worlds. Walking their dogs, chatting with their neighbors. Things slowed down a bit with the pandemic, but now everything is back to what I remember. This constant movement.

I could only imagine what this was like back in '86. My parents and my brothers landed here in a cold February. My parents, building a home so far away from Pakistan. My brothers, creating a new life for themselves without experienced guides. And I wasn't even born yet. My family managed, got through it. Like nature, anxiety and worry are always there. None of this is new.

I take a deep breath.
Stand, then begin the walk home.
One step at a time.

KI BANU DUNIYA DA

Before backing out, I connect my music.
Can you even drive a car without music?

Dhadd on wheels, percussions make my speakers Bhangra.
I introduce myself with the timbre of my music.

I'm loud because I must be heard.
Never want to silence my music.

But truthfully, I used to lower the volume.
Self-conscious about the foreign melodies of my music.

A hyphened identity is a multilingual two-sided cassette.
Side A: instructions on assimilation. Monotone music.

Side B: Too American now. Off-key pitch,
no depth in vocabulary. *Our music is not your music.*

I listened to the wrong notes.
You don't know the words, why are you even listening to this music?

Cacophonous opinions. Tumbi ka nachna, a rhythm I couldn't ignore.
Sarangi ka gaana called me, said: ghaar aa jao. Come home to music.

I'm home. Abbu's speakers say Salaam first. I hear my playlist.
Guru Randhawa, Diljit Dosanjh. Same taste in music.

I get my love for music from Abbu. He knows his history
like a vinyl record player, needle-drop-quick recall of Desi music.

After trading songs, we put on a Coke Studio throwback.
Gurdas Maan is Abbu's favorite singer. His music,

that vibrato, mastery of vocal tones. So powerful,
he introduces me to ancestors with his music.

This song, a harmony between generations. Joined by Diljit,
they ask, *what is to become of the world* if we silence our music?

Lose our sense of love, value in our traditions, pride in our languages.
Songs can reconnect us if we just listen to the music.

Still, nothing is solved with press-play. Partition a fresh wound,
trauma tender. Diaspora with dysphoria trying to define home. Music

matters but we must also agree to be in concert.
Bridges are giant harps. Wind whispers strumming cables. Music

is loud enough to cross our differences. Abbu left Pakistan
for a prosperous life in America. Opportunity, a universal music,

but so is the dhol's heartbeat frequency.
Bringing us home, together, listening to music.

As I grow older, I'm more comfortable in my ancestral tongue.
I shh out annoying background noise, focus solely on my music.

Samajtha hoon Abbu but I need help understanding some phrases.
I want to learn though. These songs move me. I love our music.

Teek hai Beta. Some people can only translate words.
They still can't feel the poetry, hear the music.

EPILOGUE

HI! MY NAME IS USMAN

Mispronounced as
Guzman or Us-man.

I was the pause during the attendance sheet reading,
the stumble after a long list of Anglo-Saxon names.
A foreign one like mine was a problem
solved by process of elimination.

I accepted this as my reality.
Actually it's Usman
was a dodged conversation.

I did not believe I was worth defending.
I bartered my culture for acceptance,
suffocated my accent in throat.
Urdu and Hindi
would double-check their visas
before flying out of my mouth.
Carry with them the baggage of being
Pakistani by heritage,
American by birth.

I never knew where I belonged.
Understood that if my name was mispronounced,
I should say nothing.
Blame the syllables but stick to the syllabus.

I am a story of many.
I know a boy born Osama.
He is now Usman;
his mother changed his name to avoid danger.
A synonym for safety,
but I wonder if Usman
sees his skin as pride or prison.

I grew up a visitor
at the museum of my ancestry.
Never felt worthy enough to enter.
Maybe I bartered too much,
gave away my identity for an acceptance
from America that was conditional at best.

I lived years like this
until I met Ashni and Wajida and Hyder—
countless others with history in their names.
Marvelous murals glowing with sooraj,
brown, bold features,
elegantly arched eyebrows, pepper-black stubble.
Children of diaspora,
they knew my story as their own.

The day I looked in a mirror and
saw kabsoorath, beautiful, in the reflection
was revival, a new existence.

It was as if they taught me to walk again.
When we danced, we moved as one.
Our Mela choreography continues to beckon my body.
My steps may not be Fresh off the Boat,
but they are the desi mere doston ne sikhaaya,
the South Asian my friends taught me.
My anthems of identity
are their spirits rewritten in rhythms
replayed on dance tracks
booming in my headphones.

I no longer avoid conversations.
I will correct you—
My name is Usman.
I was bushy eyebrows before Aubrey Graham was Drake,
and I've turned food stamps into full-tuition scholarships,
chasing down my dreams
like they were on the last train leaving for home.

So, to the boys with facial hair in 8th grade,
girls named *exotic* as if it were a compliment,
adults weighted down with assimilation,
children whose names unaccustomed mouths trip over—

our heritage is mainstream now,
but they gentrified the recipe.

Drench this melting pot
with the masala brought over
by our mothers.
Our culture is not an apology.
Thunder our ancestry,

let them hear our music.
Let them know:
we are here.
We will not be quiet.

ACKNOWLEDGMENTS

:Cue "The Avengers" by Alan Silvestri:

Thank you for reading my first book!

Staying Right Here is a journey that includes so many people. I was anxious about writing this section because I have so much gratitude to give. While I don't have the space to mention all of the people that impacted my life to reach this point, please know that your words and energy helped me craft this work. I'm grateful for you.

I'd like to first start off with my family. I love my Ammi and Abbu so much. A goal of this book was to dive into my relationship with them. This book has given me the chance to see how much they have impacted my life and the sacrifices they have made. I hope I have made you proud. I would also like to thank my brothers for their love and kindness over the years. Thank you to my niece for thinking I'm still cool. Watching you grow up is a treasure.

Thank you to Salman Hamdani and the Hamdani family. Salman, your sacrifice will always be one of the most transformative moments of my life. I'm so grateful that I got to meet you when I was so young and you were a nerdy, Young Jedi. May Allah continue to bless you.

I am fortunate to have many genuine friendships. For this book, I'd like to thank Hyder Kazmi, Ashni Davé, Wajida Syed, Miguel Vizarreta, Phillip Comella, Robert Wiener and Larissa Cao. You all gave me so many core memories and poems. Thank you for laughter and joy. Rest in Power to Verdery Knights, really wish I could've sent you my drafts, but I feel like you got to read them anyway.

Poems flourish in communities. Thank you to my Lizard family (Art, Warrior, Lexi, Alicia, Tom, Jeff, Slam Mama, Cole, and Rudy). Thank you to the Watering Hole for welcoming me in as Tribe and giving me the support I needed. Yes, I am an East Coast poet, but the South gave me the strength and courage I needed to be proud of my work. The South made me feel like I belong here.

Speaking of the South, I HAVE to show love to the King of the South him-self, Frederick "Breeze" Eberhardt. Many of the poems in this collection have come from us working, editing, and planning together in the #dojo. Having a decorated champion like Breeze believe in me has been so em-powering. But beyond his resume, Breeze continues to teach me how to be a better person. And we are just getting started! Lights, camera, action!

MID-CREDIT POEM

My journey forward
looks at the past and wishes:
so much I would change.

Wanted to stay there.
Thought that I already peaked.
My best behind me.

But now, it is done.
I have much more left to give.
New paths lie ahead.

The editing of this book was a collective effort. Thank you so much to Jason H.S. Nadelbaum, Simone Person, Omar Holmon, Jake Weiner, and Michael Mlekoday for their feedback. Special thank you to my twin Jake for being my ride-or-die since Otis. Jason, it feels like just yesterday we were rehearsing for CUPSI. Omar, I've been trying to uphold the nerd crown since I met you.

Love to the journals and platforms that have published earlier version of work featured in this collection:

"Heirloom" was published in *Intima: A Journal of Narrative Medicine.*

Earlier versions of "Hi! My Name is Usman" and "God Bless Deli Speaks to My Gentrified Neighborhood" were video published by Write About Now. Thank you to Amir Safi for being such a strong Muslim voice in slam for so long.

Earlier versions of "Flying While Muslim. Then. Now. Probably Forever," "College Admissions," and "Reflecting Pool" were video published by Button Poetry. "College Admissions" was also published by Voicemail Poems.

Speaking of Button Poetry, thanks for the book deal! Special thank you to TaneshaNicole Tyler for being such a reliable point of contact in this process. This is my first time writing a book and you were so incredibly helpful! Sam Van Cook, you were one of the first poets I met at CUPSI, back when scores were posted on walls. Can't believe our journeys are still connected!

Poems that are inspired by or include work from other artists are as follows:

"Owed to Ms. Samuel" was inspired by Dr. Joshua Bennett's book *Owed,* specifically the homophones ode and owed.

"Fragile" is based on the glass art of Simon Berger. Please check out his work and write your own ekphrastic poems!

"Hurricanes: Revisited" is from a workshop led by Paul Tran, where they used Edgar Kunz's "In the Supply Closet at Illing Middle" as a source of inspiration for the prompt that led to my poem.

"Where Are You Really From?" is after and in conversation with Carlos Andrés Gómez's "Where Are You Really From?" Thank you to Carlos for your inspiring poem and approving how I used it in my own work.

"There's No Place Like Home" is a golden shovel with lines from "The City" by Nathalie Handal. It was also published in the Worcester Review. Thank you Nathalie for your flash fiction workshop at VONA. I learned so much and your teachings helped me with the prose work in my collection.

"Questions During My First Zoom Lecture" is after Jim Moore's "Twenty Questions." Thank you Jim for this incredible form and for making my life so much easier during COVID teaching.

Thank you to the following organizations (in no particular order): Brandeis University, Mass Poetry, The Posse Foundation, Global Kids, and the Mount Sinai Hospital/the Icahn School of Medicine at Mount Sinai.

Jamele, you got a whole poem brother but it wouldn't be an acknowledgments sections without you!

Banneker. When I graduated, I had a Saul Williams scroll of folks to thank for my journey. It still holds true. You all were such an important part of my adolescence. Seeing how we grew up is beautiful. To my teachers, I didn't realize how much you all gave me in those moments. I still remember your classrooms. Special thank you to all my English teachers who helped shape this book: Ms. Samuel, Mr. Egashira, Ms. Cook, Mr. de Chalus, and Ms. Ford.

I'll take a quick moment to thank myself. As you have read in this book, there were so many moments where I could've stopped . . . writing. I'm glad I didn't.

To my beloved Nari. Even when poetry felt like an impossible goal, you saw something in me. You believed in my story. Thank you for reading all my drafts, your artistic input, and your patience during all those long nights. I loved seeing your creative genius shine during this project. These milestones are ours. Let's enjoy them together ♥

ABOUT THE AUTHOR

Photo credit: Beau

Usman Hameedi is a Pakistani-American scientist, poet, and educator. He also serves on Mass Poetry's Board of Directors. Since 2008, he has competed in and coached for collegiate, national, and international level poetry slams. Usman has been featured on *The Huffington Post*, *Intima: A Journal of Narrative Medicine*, and *The Story Collider: Storytelling for Scientists* podcast. His first full-length collection, *Staying Right Here*, is forthcoming by Button Poetry (2023). Usman was a Mass Poetry Artist-in-Residence and worked with students in Hyde Park and Salem. He has also worked with other educators on how they can incorporate poetry into their classroom communities. Usman is shaping his career around his missions and ideals. His proudest moments are helping others see the genius within themselves!

BOOK RECOMMENDATIONS FROM THE AUTHOR

The following books, also published by Button Poetry, helped me craft my book *Staying Right Here.*

Born in a Second Language by Akosua Zimba Afiriyie-Hwedie

Afiriyie-Hwedie's book pushed me to delve into my relationships with the languages that have shaped my identity. I recommend her book to anyone who is trying to bring out their authentic self in their work. Her book is also a master's class in form and formatting, exemplifying how the page is a stage to share one's story and being bold with written performance creates added layers for readers to journey through.

We Were All Someone Else Yesterday by Omar Holmon

Holmon writes in a way that makes you feel like you were there with him throughout his whole journey, for the funny times as well as the challenging ones. He can make you shed tears of joy and sorrow at the same time. From Holmon, I learned to be adventurous with my content and to not be afraid of trying new ways to share my stories. Humor is an immensely powerful tool and Holmon has been a legendary wielder of the art for decades.

BloodFresh by Ebony Stewart

Sometimes I hide behind literary devices because I'm afraid to say what I really want to. Stewart pushed to me to lay it all out there. Vulnerable and unapologetic. But once it is out there, Stewart also showed me how to dig deeper by thinking about my journey and how those different episodes have shaped who I am. I recommend her work to anyone who needs a guide on how to spill themselves onto a page. The Queen of the South is the best teacher you could ask for.

OTHER BOOKS BY BUTTON POETRY

If you enjoyed this book, please consider checking out some of our others, below. Readers like you allow us to keep broadcasting and publishing. Thank you!

Available at buttonpoetry.com/shop and more!

FORTHCOMING BOOKS BY BUTTON POETRY

Sean Patrick Mulroy, *Hated for the Gods*
Sierra DeMulder, *Ephemera*
Taylor Mali, *Poetry By Chance*
Matt Mason, *Rock Stars*
Miya Coleman, *Cotton Mouth*